Welcome RAMADAN!

Lila Assiff-Tarabain

Goodword

Illustrated by Gurmeet
First published 2008, Reprinted 2018
© Goodword Books 2018

Goodword Books
A-21, Sector 4, Noida-201301, India
Tel. +9111-46010170, +9111-49534795
Mob. +91-8588822672
email: info@goodwordbooks.com
www.goodwordbooks.com

Printed in India

Hello Moon!
What a welcome sight!
We've searched for you throughout the night.

Seeing you now, tells Muslims all
Not to eat or drink until nightfall.

For Ramadan, the month of Fast
Is here for us,

Hooray! At last!

"What is Ramadan?" Bilal asked his big sister Maysa.

Maysa smiled at her brother as she remembered what mommy and daddy told her when she asked the same question, not too long ago.

"In the special month of Ramadan, before each dawn,
Muslims, like daddy and mommy
eat some food to fill their tummies." explained Maysa.

"But when the sun is ready to rise, they will not eat, not even one bite!"

"Why can't we eat?" wondered Bilal.

"No breakfast? No Lunch? No Snacks? I'll be so hungry!"

What!
No Lunch !!!

Maysa laughed, "you and I we are still
too young to fast you know,
and we do need food to help us grow."

10

"And every day at each sunset, the fasting Muslim breaks his fast.
We break the fast on milk and dates,
then eat the meals that mommy makes."

Then every night we go to pray.
The way we do throughout the day.
We stand up tall, then bow down low
Asking God to help us all.

We do not bite, or shout, or lie.
We pray to God to help us keep our Fast,
And give us patience in every task.

13

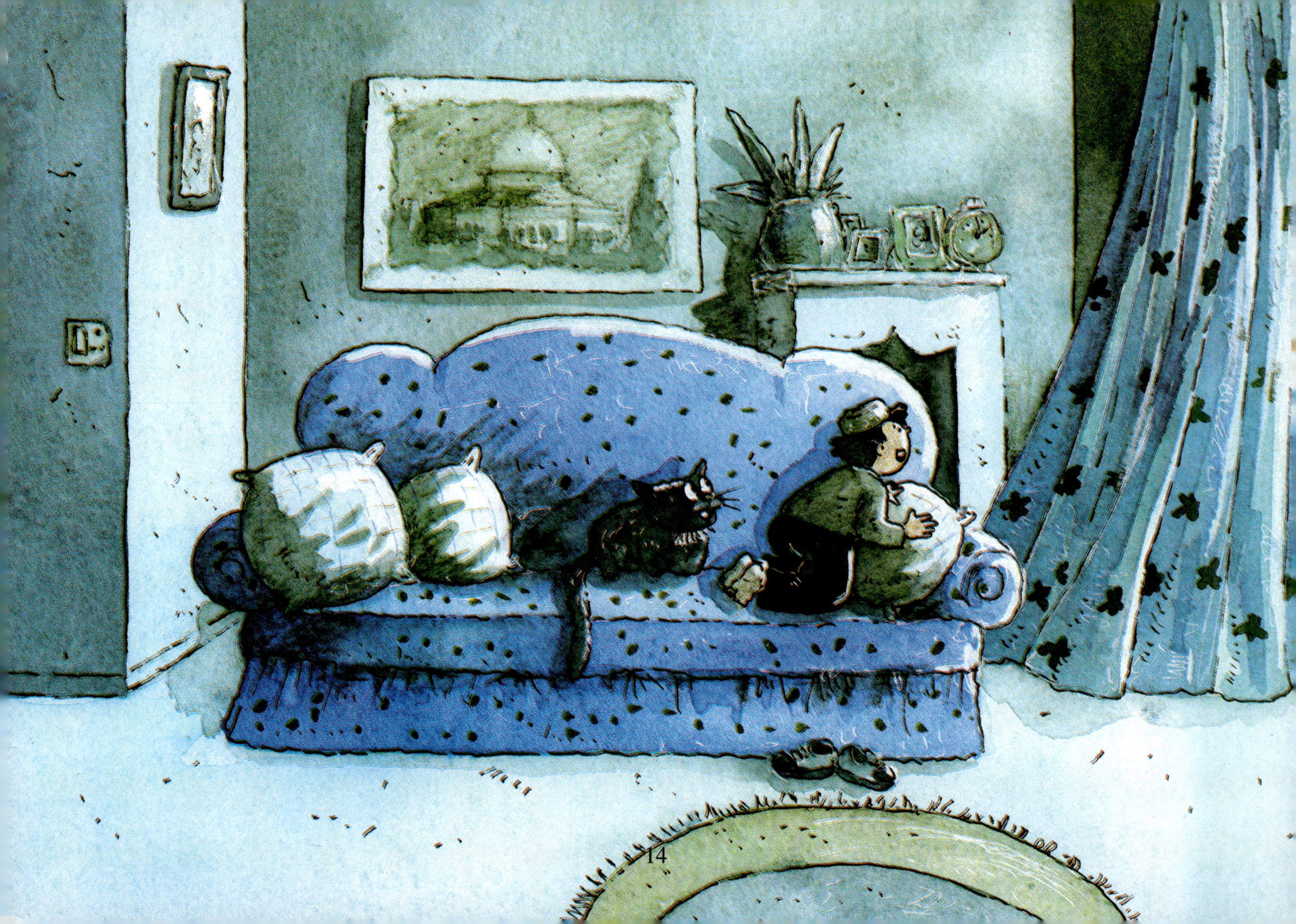

"Look, look! Bilal," exclaimed Maysa,
"do you see the moon?
So full and bright it lights the room!"

Now Ramadan is half-way done
And Eid al-Fitr will soon come!

Every day in Ramadan,
Muslims always read the Quran.

This Quran is a Holy book,
into which everyone should take a look.

The fasting Muslim gives prayers of thanks.
in the morning, noon, and late at night.

The special month of Ramadan helps us remember
to thank God for everything we have.
We may eat and drink whatever we want.

But many children around the world
go to sleep hungry and thirsty.
Day and night their tummies ache.
No bread, no rice, no frosty milkshakes.

So, especially in Ramadan,
Muslims give money and food to the poor and needy,
and never, ever hope to be greedy.

And before Ramadan slips away,
the fasting Muslim's spirit is here to stay.
To do good deeds and from bad stay clear,
each and every day of the year.

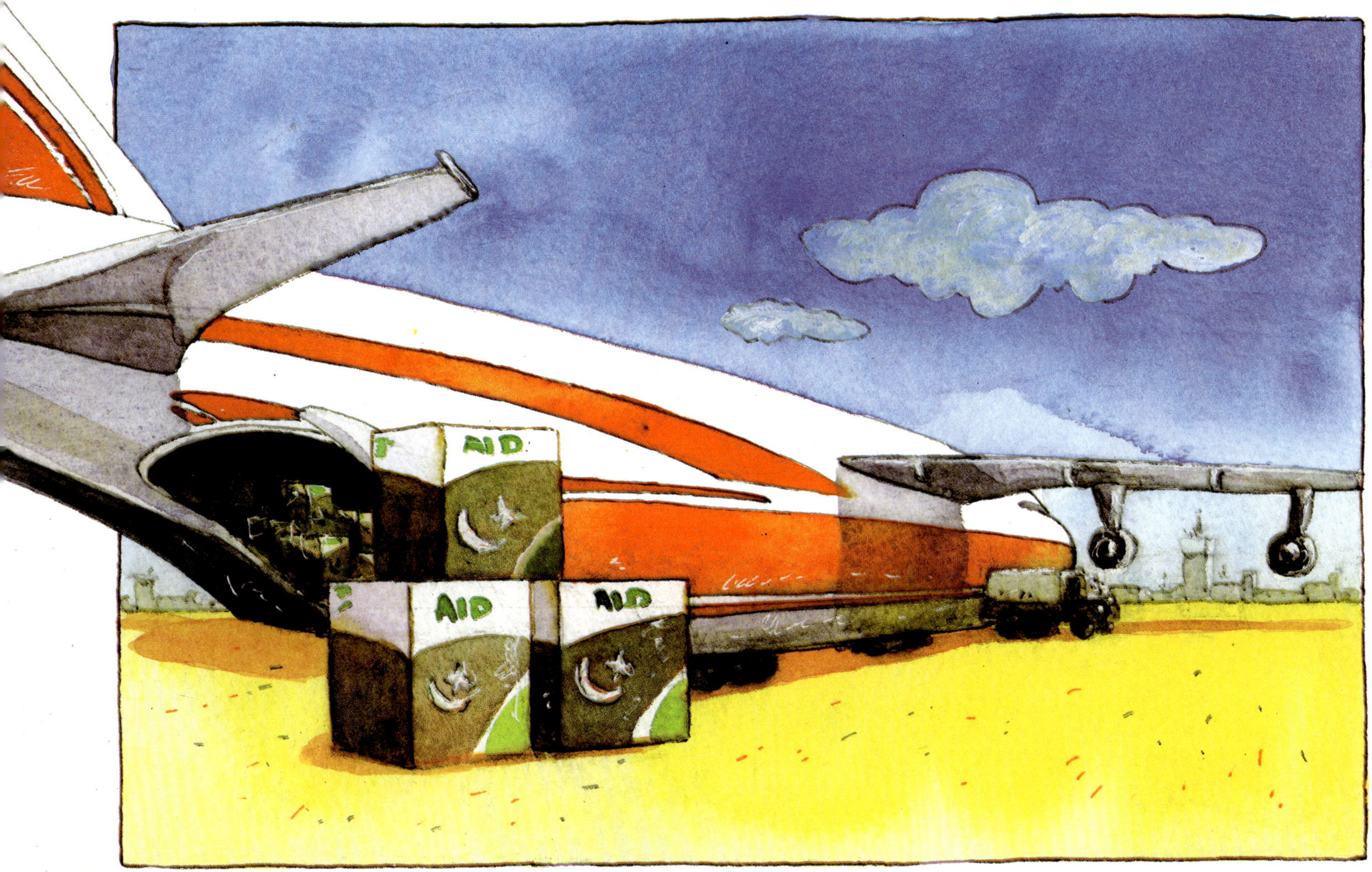
AID
AID
AID

Now the moon is a crescent again
The month of Ramadan has come to an end.

Eid al-Fitr is finally here!
We cant wait for Ramadan to come next year!

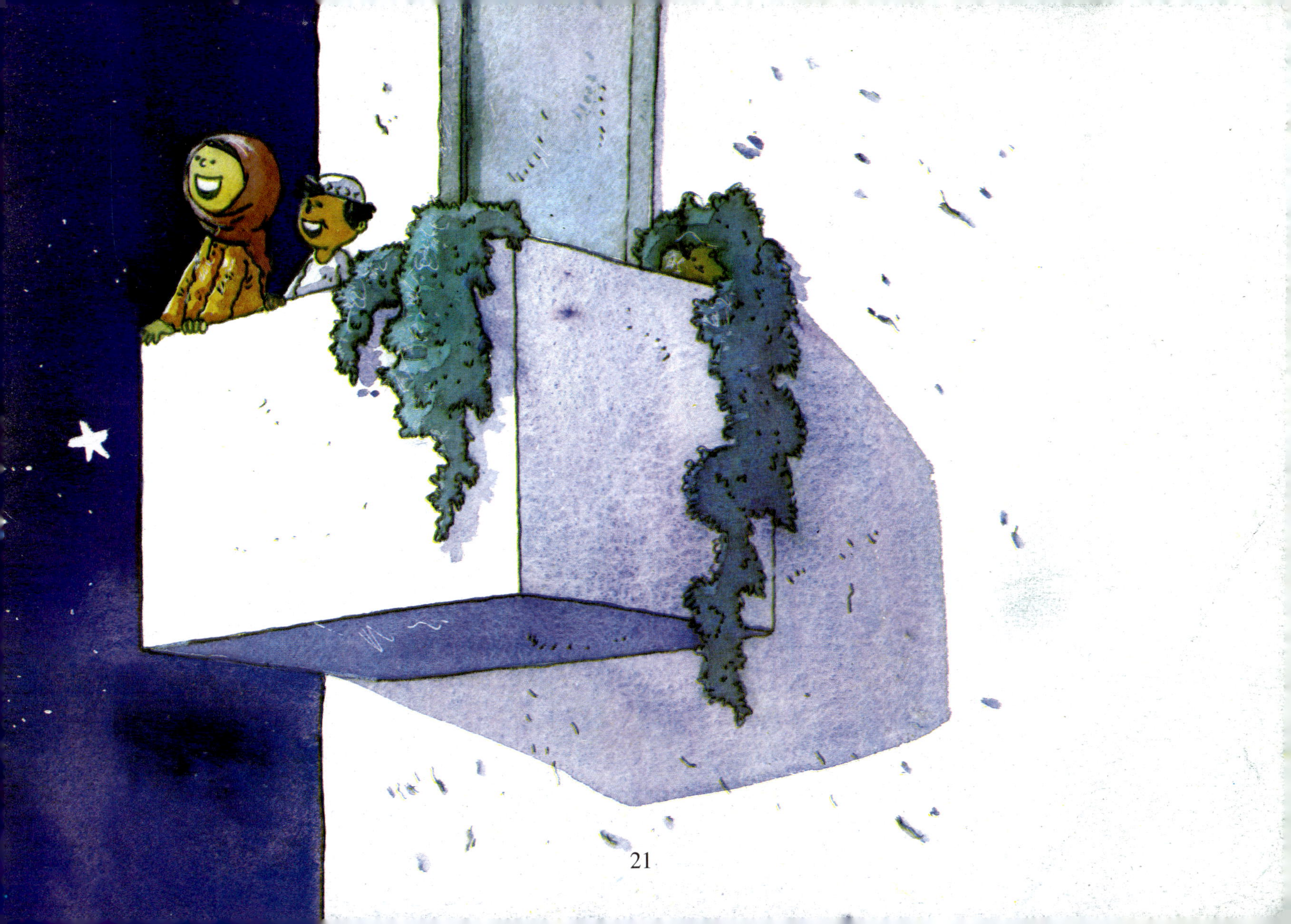

Eid

Mubarak!!!

Parent/Teacher Guide

Ramadan is the ninth month of the Islamic lunar calendar. The lunar calendar is based on the phases of the moon and has twelve lunar months. Therefore, the actual date of Ramadan changes by 11 or 12 days each solar year.

Fasting during Ramadan is one of the five pillars of Islam and is obligatory on every healthy person. Young children and people in poor health are among those that are exempt from fasting. People who cannot fast for whatever reason should make up the missed days of fasting of Ramadan on other days during the year. If they cannot do so, then they should feed the poor and needy instead.

A Muslim fasts by waking up early and eating a pre-dawn meal. Then when the sun rises, the fasting Muslim will not eat or drink until sunset. This cycle is continued for the entire month of Ramadan. During this month, the Muslim will also do his utmost to refrain from anything bad and try to do many good deeds.

The spirit of fasting in Ramadan builds human character by encouraging the person to do good and refrain from doing anything that would harm others. The fasting person learns patience, perseverance, self-discipline, sacrifice, and compassion and sympathy for those that are less fortunate.

The beginning of Ramadan is marked by the sighting of the crescent moon. It continues for twenty-nine or thirty days, depending again upon the sighting of the first crescent following the new moon. When the crescent moon is sighted and the month of Ramadan ends, Muslims celebrate with a feast called Eid-al-Fitr. It is customary to visit family, friends and neighbors during the days of Eid. Gifts are often exchanged and meals are joyously shared.

If you would like more information on Ramadan or other Islamic holidays, please do not hesitate to contact your local mosque or log on to:
www.goodwordbooks.com
www.alrisala.org, www.cpsglobal.org